For Darnell and Jalen
—E. E.

To my husband, Bagus, my children, Augurius, Alfonsus,
and Clementine... my rays of sunshine
—E. A.

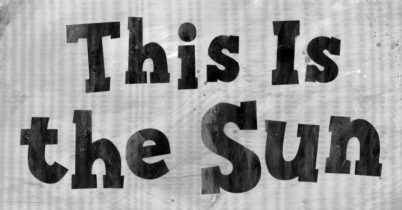

This Is the Sun

Written by **Elizabeth Everett**
Illustrated by **Evelline Andrya**

Science, Naturally!
An imprint of Platypus Media, LLC

This is the **Sun.**

This is the **light**
that comes from the Sun.

This is the **tree** that uses the light from the Sun to make its own food.

This is the **flower** that starts to bloom as it grows on the tree

that uses the light from the Sun to make its own food.

This is the **bug** that sits on a leaf and nibbles the flower

that starts to bloom as it grows on the tree
that uses the light from the Sun to make its own food.

This is the **spider** that spins its web to trap the bug

that sits on a leaf and nibbles the flower
that starts to bloom as it grows on the tree
that uses the light from the Sun to make its own food.

This is the **lizard** that flicks its tongue to catch the spider

that spins its web to trap the bug
that sits on a leaf and nibbles the flower
that starts to bloom as it grows on the tree
that uses the light from the Sun to make its own food.

This is the **snake** that snaps its jaws to grab the lizard

that flicks its tongue to catch the spider
that spins its web to trap the bug
that sits on a leaf and nibbles the flower
that starts to bloom as it grows on the tree
that uses the light from the Sun to make its own food.

This is the **fox** that sneaks on its paws to pounce on the snake

that snaps its jaws to grab the lizard
that flicks its tongue to catch the spider
that spins its web to trap the bug
that sits on a leaf and nibbles the flower
that starts to bloom as it grows on the tree
that uses the light from the Sun to make its own food.

This is the **scat** that falls to the ground at the feet of the fox

that sneaks on its paws to pounce on the snake
that snaps its jaws to grab the lizard
that flicks its tongue to catch the spider
that spins its web to trap the bug
that sits on a leaf and nibbles the flower
that starts to bloom as it grows on the tree
that uses the light from the Sun to make its own food.

This is the **seed** that comes from the tree and lands in the scat

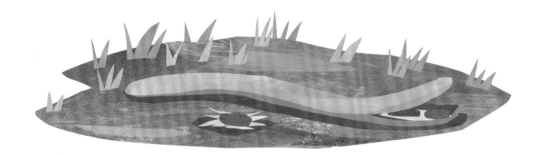

that falls to the ground at the feet of the fox
that sneaks on its paws to pounce on the snake
that snaps its jaws to grab the lizard
that flicks its tongue to catch the spider
that spins its web to trap the bug
that sits on a leaf and nibbles the flower
that starts to bloom as it grows on the tree
that uses the light from the Sun to make its own food.

This is the **sprout**
that grows from the seed
and reaches toward the Sun...

and this is the **Sun**
that brings the circle to life.

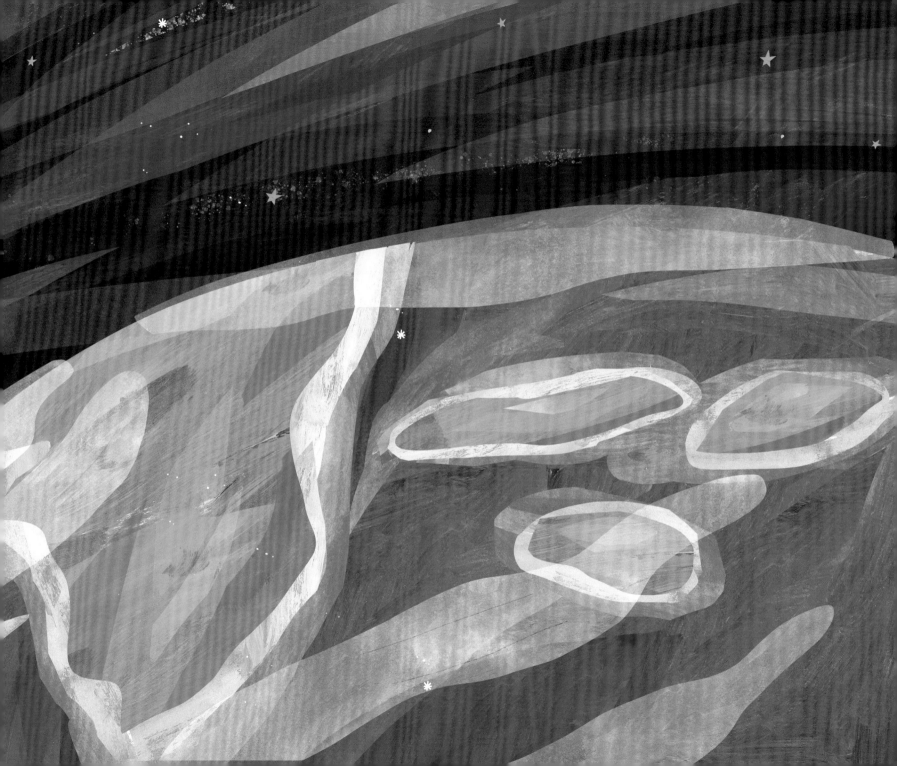

Meet the Author and Illustrator

Elizabeth Everett spent 16 years as a classroom teacher before venturing into writing. Inspired by her energetic youngster, Jalen, and his love for books, she took her background in education and meshed it with his childhood interests. The result was edu-tainment in the form of children's books! She currently lives in Colorado with her family where they love spending time outdoors in the Western sun. This is her first children's book and she is excited to have several more coming out soon. She can be reached at Elizabeth.Everett@ScienceNaturally.com.

Evelline Andrya was born in Sumatra, Indonesia. She grew up with both Chinese and Javanese cultures. Her passion in illustration started at a very young age. She was influenced by vintage greeting cards that she found in her grandma's drawer, comic books, antique picture books, and animated movies. Her illustration style is a mix of traditional medium and digital collage. She lives in Jakarta with her husband and three children. Find her on Instagram @evellineandrya.

This Is the Sun
Hardcover first edition • October 2022 • ISBN: 978-1-938492-81-5
Paperback first edition • October 2022 • ISBN: 978-1-938492-82-2
eBook first edition • October 2022 • ISBN: 978-1-938492-83-9

Written by Elizabeth Everett, Text © 2022
Illustrated by Evelline Andrya, Illustrations © 2022

Project Manager, Cover and Book Design: Caitlin Burnham, Washington, D.C.
Editors:
Marlee Brooks, Chevy Chase, MD
Hannah Thelen, Silver Spring, MD
Editorial Assistants:
Caitlin Chang, Sienna Sullivan, Amara Leonard

Available in Spanish as Este es el Sol
Spanish Paperback first edition • October 2022 • ISBN: 978-1-938492-84-6
Spanish eBook first edition • October 2022 • ISBN: 978-1-938492-85-3

Teacher's Guide available at the Educational Resources page of ScienceNaturally.com

Published by:
　　Science, Naturally! – An imprint of Platypus Media, LLC
　　750 First Street NE, Suite 700
　　Washington, DC 20002
　　202-465-4798 • Fax: 202-558-2132
　　Info@ScienceNaturally.com • ScienceNaturally.com

Distributed to the book trade by:
　　National Book Network (North America)
　　　　301-459-3366 • Toll-free: 800-462-6420
　　　　CustomerCare@NBNbooks.com • NBNbooks.com
　　NBN International (worldwide)
　　　　NBNi.Cservs@IngramContent.com • Distribution.NBNi.co.uk

Library of Congress Control Number: 2022935511

10 9 8 7 6 5 4 3 2 1

Printed in China.